A
VILLAGE CALLED
HOPE

BEVERLEE McGRATH

Library of Congress Control Number: 2024927099

ISBN: 979-8-89228-399-1   (Paperback)
ISBN: 979-8-89228-400-4   (Hardcover)
ISBN: 979-8-89228-401-1   (eBook)

Printed in the United States of America

My heartfelt thanks go to Rodney and Heather Croston, whose warmth and laughter over dinner helped inspire the words for this book. Your encouragement and thoughtful insights made the writing process a joy. A special thank you to my first cousin, Bonnie Westmark, for your unwavering support and belief in this project— you've been a true cheerleader throughout this journey. This book wouldn't be what it is without all of you.

THE JOURNEY

The wind was soft, the path was clear, and the sun was starting to show.

They'd packed a lunch and started their trip, they'd planned a walk very slow.

Stumpy's leg wouldn't work, goodness only knows
why, and poor Cleo couldn't see.

She'd been trapped in a barn, the fire spread from
the house, the Doctor helped her and said,

"Oh Goodness Me!"

Doc said she'd never see, she was fine otherwise, it was lucky she was able to break down the gate.

"I want to help them", Cowboy said to the air, "We'll leave it to spirits and fate".

It seems Stumpy, the goat, Cleo, the pig, and
Cowboy, the pony, all had a special dream.

Where they ran through the meadows, over the hills,
and rode on a sparkling beam.

They dreamt of a village where fairies lived, but
never knew where it could be.

Where fairies make Magic, their Magic is real, it's the
Magic all three want to see.

Where Stumpy can walk and climb stairs, Cleo can
see and play.

Cowboy will feel better and frolic throughout
the day.

Today seemed the day when all things can happen,
they'd follow the beam from the sun.

They'd look for the fairies, walk slowly and hope,
Yes, today they'll be able to run.

FINDING FAIRYLAND

They remembered the wise barn owl's recipe - for finding the Fairyland:

A full heart of HOPE,

Half teaspoon of FUN,

Cupful of LOVE

Then wave the wand in your hand

They never doubted that there was a place where fairies and dreams are true,

"It's inside of one's mind", said the wise owl, "and happiness follows on cue."

THE ANIMAL SPIRIT

The sun took a turn, but they followed the beam, and
the white fluffy clouds were a sight.

The butterflies danced, the bees hummed a song,
they hoped to reach fairies that night.

They continued to walk, but Cowboy grew tired, so they decided to rest by a stream.

"We could turn around and go back to the farm, but then we'd give up on our dream!"

On and on they walked and Stumpy began to say:
"Everything's smaller, really small -I wonder just
who could live here?"

The trees were short, the roads were paths, the
butterflies tiny, but dear.

Up the hill and over the bridge, a road sign showed
where the fairies are.

They'd walked so long, hope was near, and actually,
wasn't that far.

Her wings sparkled so, she had many friends joining
in, as she came out of the tree

"What do you want?", the small fairy asked, "And
who do you wish to see?"

"We're looking for magic, we all need your help,
we've come a very long way."

"We've nothing to give in return but LOVE," was all
that Cleo could say."

The small fairy smiled and gave Cleo a wink, "The
ANIMAL SPIRIT is near."

"Take the road called PERSISTENCE to the village of
HOPE, the ANIMAL SPIRIT is here."

"Ask the dogs for directions, they'll show you the way." The
big, brownish dog did just that.

He was gray on his face, had a stiff-legged gait, but
happy when they gave him a pat.

The small fairy left, walking backwards it seemed,
she walked differently, that's for sure.

Stumpy never forgot her, copied her gait, for walking
a different way was his cure.

They followed her directions, followed the dog, and
finally arrived at Hope

Cowboy was eating hay in a field, refusing to leave,
and Cleo had to pull on his rope.

THE ANIMAL SPIRIT

They were all nervous and didn't know what to say.

They hoped he would listen and help them, and not
just send them on their way.

Cowboy went first, Stumpy wanted to wait, Cleo
said she'd go after Cowboy spoke.

Cowboy walked up slowly, explained his poor
health, waited for Cleo and gave her a poke!

The Animal Spirit was patient and very kind
to the three,

I'm always with you, helping in different ways,
so never, ever, be afraid of me.

They all felt that SOMETHING happened at HOPE,
they felt that for sure.

Cleo was first to say, "I really think he
gave me a cure!"

Stumpy walked backwards, Cleo's vision improved.

Cowboy had more energy when eating proper food.

Their friendship and persistence had
taught them to cope.

Together they walked home from
the village of HOPE.

REAL LIFE PICTURES OF PICTURES OF COWBOY, STUMPY AND CLEO.

A VILLAGE CALLED "HOPE"

Cowboy's owners were charged with neglect and he was taken away from them. After years of little or no food and no regular care, he was put on a high protein diet with vitamins. His energy increased and he is a healthy pony.

Stumpy was brought to the sanctuary with a crippled front leg; he walked with difficulty and was unable to climb stairs. He practiced, and is now able to walk and climb stairs backwards.

Cleo was trapped in a barn during the horrible "Thomas Fire" in Ventura County and she was blinded.

The Veterinarian said she would NEVER regain her eyesight. But miraculously - she did! She now lives on the McGrath Ranch - Crops and Critters, an animal sanctuary and plays with the other animals.

ABOUT THE AUTHOR

Beverlee's journey from a humble farm in Washington to becoming a champion for animal rights is nothing short of inspiring. Growing up surrounded by pigs, chickens, and a beloved pet cow named Lady, Beverlee couldn't ignore the profound emotions these animals displayed during difficult times. It was this early realization that sparked her lifelong commitment to making a difference in the lives of animals.

With determination and passion, Beverlee carved out a successful career as a lobbyist for national animal organizations, tirelessly advocating for laws to better protect and care for animals across the country. But her dedication didn't stop there. Now residing on a sprawling strawberry ranch, Beverlee has transformed her passion into action by establishing "Crops and Critters," an extraordinary farm animal rescue facility.

At "Crops and Critters," Beverlee opens her heart and home to farm animals in need, offering them a second chance at life and love. But it's not just the animals who benefit from Beverlee's compassion. Through educational tours designed for school children, Beverlee shares her love for animals and fosters empathy and understanding among the next generation.

In her own words, Beverlee explains, "I noticed that children with special needs would stand away from their group and gravitate to the special needs animals like Tiny Timm. This book is for them." With warmth and sincerity, Beverlee invites readers of all ages to join her on a heartwarming journey of compassion, resilience, and the extraordinary bond between humans and animals.